All about

Plants in Spring

by Martha E. H. Rustad

Consulting Editor: Gail Saunders-Smith, PhD

Consultant: John D. Krenz, PhD
Department of Biological Sciences
Minnesota State University, Mankato

CAPSTONE PRESS
a capstone imprint

Pebble Plus is published by Capstone Press,
1710 Roe Crest Drive, North Mankato, Minnesota 56003.
www.capstonepub.com

Library of Congress Cataloging-in-Publication Data
Rustad, Martha E. H. (Martha Elizabeth Hillman), 1975-
 Plants in spring / by Martha E.H. Rustad.
   p. cm. — (Pebbles plus. All about spring)
 Includes bibliographical references and index.
ISBN 978-1-4296-8656-3 (library binding)
ISBN 978-1-4296-9362-2 (paperback)
ISBN 978-1-62065-288-6 (ebook PDF)
1. Plants—Juvenile literature. 2. Botany—Juvenile literature. 3. Spring—Juvenile literature. I. Title.

QK49.R86 2013
580—dc23

2012000292

Editorial Credits
Shelly Lyons, editor; Bobbie Nuytten, designer; Svetlana Zhurkin, photo researcher: Kathy McColley,
    production specialist

Photo Credits
Dreamstime: Hansenn, 1, Puchan, 14–15, Sergey Ovsyannikov, 10–11, Vikrant Deshpande, cover,
Witold Krasowski, 6–7; Shutterstock: Danil Vitalevich Chepko, 4–5, Fotokostic, 12–13, Katrina Leigh, 8–9,
Konkolas, 16–17, Marish (green leaf), cover and throughout, mypokcik, 20–21, Stefan Fierros, 18–19,
Zubada (leaf pattern), cover

Note to Parents and Teachers

The All about Spring series supports national science and social studies standards related to
changes during the seasons. This book describes and illustrates plants in spring. The images
support early readers in understanding the text. The repetition of words and phrases helps early
readers learn new words. This book also introduces early readers to subject-specific vocabulary
words, which are defined in the Glossary section. Early readers may need assistance to read
some words and to use the Table of Contents, Glossary, Read More, Internet Sites, and Index
sections of the book.

Printed in the United States   4301

Table of Contents

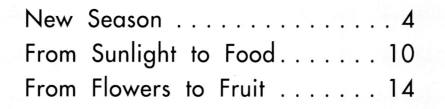

New Season

It's spring.

We plant seeds and wait

for sunlight and rain.

Spring rain makes

the ground wet.

Plant roots suck up water

from the soil.

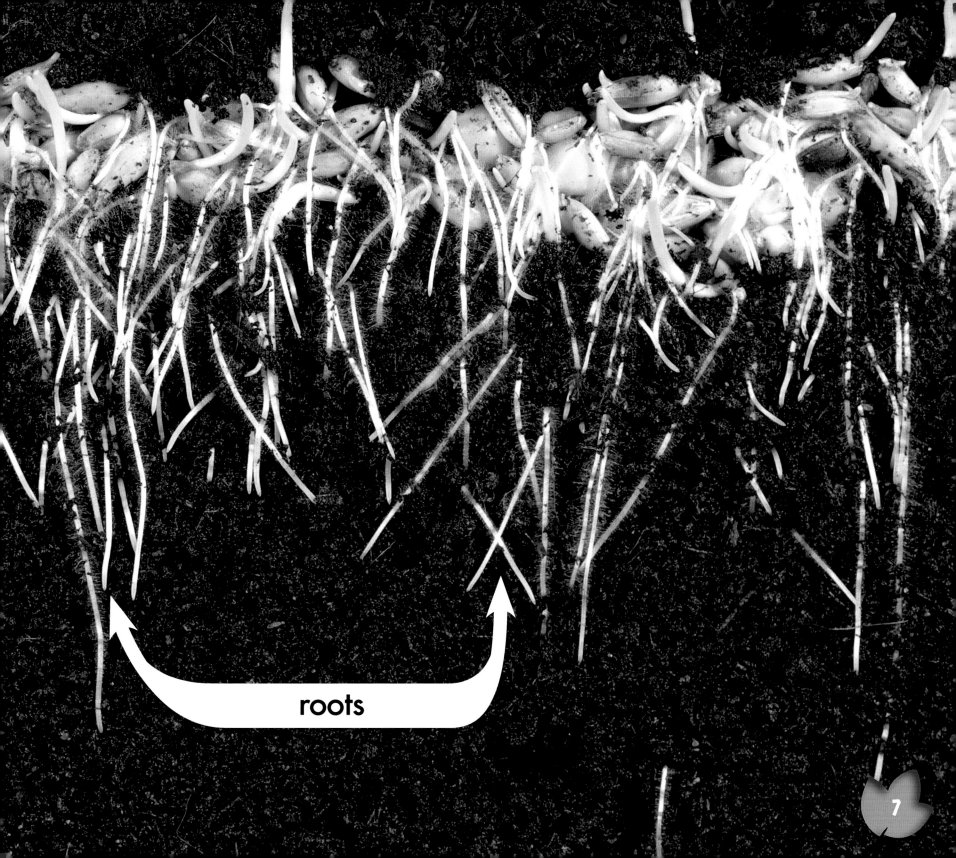

roots

Soon shoots and stems poke
through the soil.

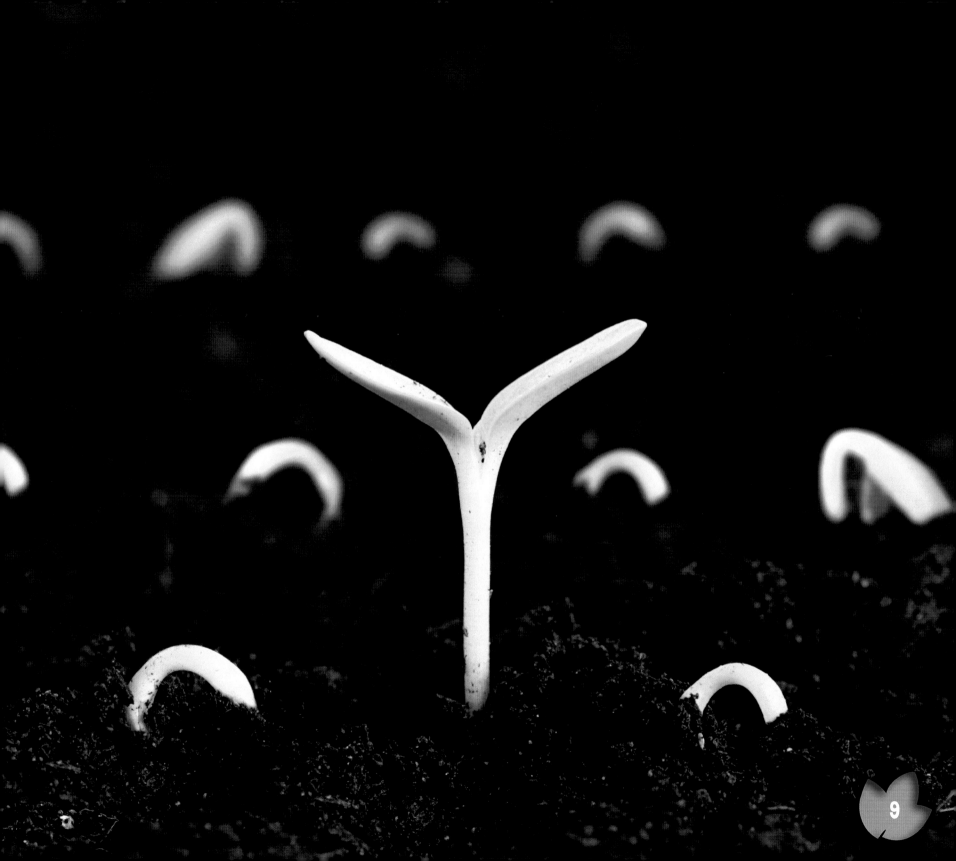

From Sunlight to Food

Daylight lasts longer

in spring.

Leaves take in the sunlight.

Plants make their own food
with sunlight, water, air,
and nutrients.

From Flowers to Fruit

Bees like bright blooming flowers.

Bees gather nectar
from the flowers.

Pollen from flowers sticks

to bees.

Bees carry the pollen

from flower to flower.

pollen

Soon flowers make fruits.

New seeds grow

inside the fruits.

Spring is a season

for planting and growing.

What plants do you see

in spring?

Glossary

bloom—to flower

fruit—the fleshy, juicy part of a plant that contains seeds and usually can be eaten

nectar—a sweet liquid that some insects collect from flowers and eat as food

nutrient—a substance needed by a living thing to stay healthy

pollen—tiny, yellow grains in flowers; some insects eat pollen

root—the part of a plant that grows underground; roots bring water into plants

seed—the part of a plant from which a new plant can grow

shoot—a plant that is just beginning to grow

stem—the part of a plant from which leaves and flowers grow

Read More

Anderson, Sheila M. *Spring.* Seasons. Minneapolis: Lerner Publications, 2010.

Ghigna, Charles. *I See Spring.* I See. Mankato, Minn.: Picture Window Books, 2012.

Sohn, Emily, and Erin Ash Sullivan. *New Plants: Seeds in the Soil Patch.* iScience Reader. Chicago: Norwood House Press, 2012.

Internet Sites

FactHound offers a safe, fun way to find Internet sites related to this book. All of the sites on FactHound have been researched by our staff.

Here's all you do:

Visit *www.facthound.com*

Type in this code: 9781429686563

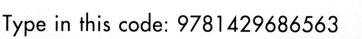
Super-cool stuff!
Check out projects, games and lots more at
www.capstonekids.com

23

Index

Word Count: 104
Grade: 1
Early-Intervention Level: 12

24